D1707067

EARLY NINETEENTH-CENTURY
CRAFTS AND TRADES

EARLY NINETEENTH-CENTURY
CRAFTS AND TRADES

Edited, with a New Introduction, by
PETER STOCKHAM

DOVER PUBLICATIONS, INC.
NEW YORK

Copyright © 1992 by Dover Publications, Inc.
All rights reserved under Pan American and International Copyright Conventions.

Published in Canada by General Publishing Company, Ltd., 30 Lesmill Road, Don Mills, Toronto, Ontario.
Published in the United Kingdom by Constable and Company, Ltd., 3 The Lanchesters, 162–164 Fulham Palace Road, London W6 9ER.

This Dover edition, first published in 1992, is an unabridged republication of Part III of the work as published by Jacob Johnson in Whitehall (Philadelphia) and Richmond in 1807 under the title *The Book of Trades, or Library of the Useful Arts*. A new Introduction has been written by Peter Stockham specially for the Dover edition.

Manufactured in the United States of America
Dover Publications, Inc., 31 East 2nd Street, Mineola, N.Y. 11501

Library of Congress Cataloging in Publication Data

Book of trades, or, Library of the useful arts. Part 3.
    Early nineteenth-century crafts and trades / edited, with a new introduction, by Peter Stockham. — Dover ed.
        p.   cm.
    "Unabridged republication of part III of the work as published by Jacob Johnson in Whitehall (Philadelphia) and Richmond in 1807 under the title: The book of trades, or Library of the useful arts."
    ISBN 0-486-27293-1 (pbk.)
    1. Industrial arts. 2. Occupations—Early works to 1900.   I. Stockham, Peter.   II. Title.
T47.B7225   1992
670—dc20   92-40610
                                                CIP

INTRODUCTION

TO THE DOVER EDITION

———•———

The third volume of *The Book of Trades, or Library of the Useful Arts* was first published in London by Benjamin Tabart in 1804 or early in 1805. The first American edition, reprinted here, appeared in 1807. Together, the three volumes* provide the most comprehensive guide to the trades practiced in the early years of the nineteenth century. Many of these trades and their operation will be familiar to the modern reader, and all are described in such detail that it seems possible to reproduce their working even today.

Much social and industrial history is to be found among the numerous descriptions of trades, lightened by the ability of the author to tell a good story. The section on the stocking weaver is an excellent example of the author's technique. Originally stockings were made of cloth or other material sewed together; it was the invention of knit-

---

*The two previous volumes are available from Dover, Part I under the title *Early American Crafts and Trades* (0-486-23336-7) and Part II under the title *Old-Time Crafts and Trades* (0-486-27398-9).

ting that gave rise to the stocking weaver. First, we learn of the introduction of knit stockings into England from Spain. This is followed by a description of the development of the knitting machine, including the romantic story of the Oxford student who lost his fellowship by marrying an innkeeper's daughter. Watching his wife knitting stockings for sale (for they were now very poor), he devised a machine that would do it more quickly, thus inventing the stocking loom. We are then told that stockings are a considerable export trade. The nature of the relationship between the master and the journeyman is also touched upon. The journeyman was paid a piece rate for each pair of stockings made, according to its fineness and complexity. If he had no loom of his own, he was allowed to hire one from his master for two shillings a week. The Scotch, we learn, were said to make the best hand-knit stockings in Europe, and they were correspondingly expensive, selling for from 30 shillings to £4 or £5 a pair.

The carpet weaver is treated in a similar way. Along with the details of the craft, we are also told that, to the credit of "the liberality and public spirit of the dissenters" of the area, an "Orphan Working School" had been set up in the City-road to weave cheap carpets from strips of cloth.

The price of the product does not appear to relate to the number of people involved in making it, although the price must, to some degree, reflect the scale of the operation. It was estimated, for example, that in the case of pin-making, twenty-five workmen were employed in the making and distribution of each pin, from the drawing of the brass wire to the sticking of the pin in the paper.

Other operations, such as tin-plate making, employed a considerable number of workers. Two firms in London employed from 100 to 150 workers each, thus incurring a considerable wages bill. Running such a large business required a very great deal of capital and meant having to sell one's products over a wide area. To do this, larger firms employed traveling salesmen who covered sales areas on horseback, carrying drawings of the firm's products in their saddlebags.

Some of the trades are now little known, although they still exist. The cork cutter still produces corks for stopping bottles, but in the account in this volume (page 124), cork is also used to make floats used in teaching young people to swim (you can see the floats hanging from the ceiling in the illustration), in waistcoats for sea bathers and those who travel by sea, and in the inner soles of shoes. Cork also had numerous other applications, such as for paints and for a medicine.

The trades are in no particular order, but related trades are grouped. In this volume, for example, trades dealing with the book are together. The papermaker is followed by the printer, and the printer by the bookbinder.

The printer in the book uses a wooden press similar to the presses that printed the first books. No mention is made of the ironclad press introduced in England a few years previously. This press was much stronger and had greater stability, and a whole sheet of paper could be printed with one pass through the machine. However, the description of the ordinary wooden press and its workings is easy to follow and shows the various actions of printing in some detail. The illustration shows the printer at work, with the composer of type making up a page in the background. The bookbinder is shown binding a book in a traditional leather binding. It was not until the 1820s and

30s that books were first bound in cloth and cased in the way a modern book is bound. Here we can see how it is done by hand, one book at a time. It is a complicated process to describe in words, but the text succeeds in making the whole complex operation easy to understand.

We tend to read these descriptions with the background of our own experience, and it is difficult for us to remember the limitations under which these crafts were carried out. Since there was no electric light, close work could often be done only in daylight, and the length of that daylight varied considerably with the time of year. Candles, although available, were quite expensive, and the danger of fire was very real and often disastrous, wiping out whole families. There must have been a high incidence of industrial accidents.

Against a background of low pay and poor working conditions, it is amazing how many skilled artisans in the early part of the nineteenth century were able to exercise such a variety of complex operations.

PETER STOCKHAM
October 1992

CONTENTS

OF

PART III.

———◆———

*** There is a Plate to each Trade.

†This illustration does not appear in the copy
being reprinted nor in any copy known to us.

BOOK OF TRADES.

THE BRICK-MAKER.

THE business of a brickmaker is carried on in the open fields, and its mode of operation may be seen in the neighbourhood of most large towns. The art in almost all its branches is regulated by different acts of parliament; and bricks may be made of pure clay, or of clay mixed in certain proportions with sand or ashes.

The clay is first moistened and tempered with water, either by the hand, or by means of a machine or mill worked with one or more horses. When it is fit for moulding into bricks, several

persons are usually, in the neighbourhood of London, employed upon the
business of making a single brick; these
are called a gang: they consist of one
or two men, a woman, and two children, to each of which is assigned a
different department in the occupation.
A gang in full work will make many
thousand bricks in the course of a single week.

In the plate the man only is represented in the act of moulding the clay
into the shape of a brick: he stands
under a sort of thatched cover to keep
off the sun and the rain; on the board
before him are all his implements; the
mould into which the clay is put, the
clay itself, which is brought to him by
another person, a vessel with some water, and a little heap of sand; and on
his left hand lies the ruler with which

Brick Maker.

he takes off the superfluous clay from the mould.

The inside of the box or mould is exactly the shape and size of a brick: the workman throws the clay into this with some violence, having first scattered a little sand about the sides of it; and then scraping off the superfluous clay, he lifts up the mould, and between two small boards conveys it to the barrow which stands near him on the ground. When the barrow is loaded another person comes and wheels away the bricks, and piles them up in an open place to dry. When the pile is made of the proper height he covers them with long straw, so that they may dry gradually without being exposed to the direct rays of the sun, which would crack them. Heavy rains would also be injurious to them; these are likewise kept off by the straw. As soon as they are sufficiently dry for the purpose they are to be burnt in a kiln. Here great art is required in piling the bricks, so that the fire may circulate through every course and in all directions. Breeze, that is, small cinders from sea-coal, is the fuel used in burning bricks, and when once well lighted it will keep burning several days till the bricks are completely finished.

Bricks when finished are of different colours, according to the clay of which they are made, but they must be all of one size; namely, nine inches long, four inches broad, and two inches and a half thick. A heavy duty is charged upon every thousand bricks; of course this business affords a large revenue to government.

The most beautiful white bricks made in this country are manufactured at Woolpit in Suffolk; these are brought by means of water carriage to all parts of England where great neatness in brickwork is an object.

A gang of brick-makers will earn a handsome living : sometimes it happens that the whole gang consists of branches of the same family, as the father and mother, and four or five children of different ages ; these will earn from two to three guineas a week ; but they work many hours, and their labour is very hard.

In connection with the trade of brick-making we must notice the manufacture of tiles, which is a sort of thin brick, made use of in the roofs of houses, and also, when something thicker, for the purposes of paving. Those for covering the roofs of houses are of different shapes, according to the uses for which they are intended ; these are plain tiles, ridge-tiles, gutter-tiles, pan-tiles, &c.

They are all made according to certain gauges, and the makers are subject to heavy penalties if their tiles exceed the dimensions fixed on by the several acts of parliament. The kilns in which tiles are burnt are large conical buildings : in these the tiles are piled from the bottom to the top before the fire is lighted. A very large manufactory of this sort is situated near Bagnigge Wells.

Flemish or Dutch tiles, which are glazed and painted, were formerly much used in chimney-jaumbs. Some thirty or forty years ago it was not uncommon to see a complete scripture history, and other curious devices, in a parlour fire-place.

THE ROPE-MAKER.

ROPE-MAKING is an art of very great importance; for without the assistance of strings, cords, ropes, cables, &c. a very small part of the business of life could be carried on that is now transacted.

Ropes of all kinds are made of hemp, twisted or spun something after the same manner of spinning wool; and the places in which ropes are manufactured are called rope-walks. These are a quarter of a mile or more in length, in the open air, but usually covered over with a slight shed to keep the workmen from the inclemencies and changes of the weather.

At the upper end of the rope-walk is a spinning-wheel, which is turned round by a person who sits on a stool or bench for the purpose : the man who forms the rope or string has a bundle of dressed hemp, such as that which lies on the truck in the plate, round his waist.   From this he draws out two or more ends and fixes them to a hook : the wheel is now turned by which the threads are twisted, and as the spinner walks backward, the rope, or more properly the rope-yarn, is lengthened. The part already twisted draws along with it more fibres out of the bundle, and the spinner gives assistance to it with his fingers, supplying hemp in due proportion as he walks away from the wheel, and taking care that the fibres come in equally from both sides of his bundle, and that they enter always with their ends, and not by the middle, which would double them. The arrangement of the fibres and the degree of twisting depend on the skill and dexterity of the

Rope Maker.

spinner. The degree of twist depends on the rate of the wheel's motion, combined with the retrograde motion of the spinner.

As soon as he is arrived at the lower end of the walk he calls out, and another spinner immediately detaches the yarn from the hook of the wheel, gives it to a third person, who takes it to the reel, and the second spinner attaches his own hemp to the whirl-hook. In the mean time the first spinner keeps fast hold of the end of his yarn, to prevent its untwisting, and as soon as the reeler begins to turn his reel, he goes slowly up the walk, keeping the yarn of an equal tightness all the way, till he arrives at the wheel, where he waits with his yarn in hand till another has finished his yarn. The first spinner takes it off the whirl-hook, joins it to his own, that it may follow it on the reel, and begins a new yarn himself.

The fibres of hemp are thus twisted into yarns, and make a line of any length : down the rope-walk are a number of upright posts with long pegs fixed in them at right angles ; on these pegs the spinner throws the rope-yarn as he proceeds, to prevent its swagging.

As many fibres are made into one yarn, so many yarns are afterward made into one rope, according to the size and strength required.   By this process, which is called *laying*, it acquires a so-lidity and hardness which render it less penetrable by water, that would rot it in a short time.

Sometimes the union of several yarns is called a strand, and a larger rope may be formed of two or more of these strands ; and in this manner cables and other ground tackle are commonly made.

Cables and cords are frequently tar-red, which is usually done in the state of yarn, this being the only method that the hemp can be uniformly penetrated. The yarn is made to wind off from one reel, and having passed through a vessel containing hot tar, it is wound up on another, and the superfluous tar is taken off by passing through a hole surrounded with spungy oakum; or it is sometimes tarred in skains or hauls, which are drawn by a capstan through the tar-kettle, and through a hole formed of two plates of metal.

It is a fact, however, that tarred cordage is very much weaker than white; it is also less pliable and less durable; but the use of tar is nevertheless necessary to defend the cordage from the action of the water.

Nets are made with small cords; larger ones are used for tying up packages; and ropes of all sizes and dimensions are used for shipping. A ship's cable is sometimes several hundred yards in length, and is worth a large sum of money.

The master rope-maker requires a considerable capital if his business is carried on upon a large scale, and a journeyman will earn with ease from a guinea to a guinea and a half a week, or even more if he is sober and industrious.

Yarn for sail-cloth is made of dressed hemp, and spun in the same manner that rope-yarn is spun. The spinners of this may make a good living; women are chiefly employed in it. The person who shapes and sews together the cloth into sails is called a sail-maker, and is sometimes denominated a ship's taylor.

THE WEAVER.

In the plate we have a good representation of a weaver engaged in his business. He sits at his work, and makes use of his feet as well as his hands. Weaving is a very extensive trade, and is divided into a multitude of different branches, such as the broad and narrow weavers. The broad weaver is employed in stuffs, broad-cloths, woollen goods, &c. the narrow weaver, in ribbons, tapes, and such other things; and there are engine looms for making some of these narrow goods, by which ten or twelve pieces can be made at once: but goods made in this way are generally not so good as those made by hand, because it is not possible to find thread in every part equal: but the engines give an equal pressure upon all threads, while the workman, weaving by hand, increases or diminishes the strength of his pull according to the quality of the thread, and by that method conceals all difference in the warp.

Linen and woollen cloth are both woven the same way; the one from thread, the other from worsted. So also is silk, which, when taken from the silk-worm, and wound, is called floss silk, and afterwards spun into sewing-silk.

The weaver sits at his *loom:* this is à machine by which several distinct threads of any kind are woven into one piece. They are of various structures, according to the several kinds of materials to be woven and to the methods of weaving them. The other principal things to be noticed are the *warp,* the *woof,* and the *shuttle.*

The *warp* is the threads, whether of silk, wool, linen, or cotton, that are extended lengthwise on the loom.

Weaver.

The *woof* is the thread which the weaver shoots across the warp, by means of a little instrument called a *shuttle*.

The *shuttle* serves to form the woof by being thrown alternately from right to left, and from left to right, across and between the threads of the warp. In the middle of the shuttle is a cavity called the eye or chamber, and in this is enclosed the spole or bobbin, on which the thread or part of it is wound.

The ribbon-weaver's shuttle is different from that of most other weavers, though it serves for the same purpose. It is made of box, and is six or seven inches long, shod with iron at both ends, which terminate in points that are crooked, one towards the right, the other towards the left.

In the front of the plate stands the reel, by means of which the thread is wound on the bobbins that lie in the wooden bowl, ready for the weaver as he wants them. The thread for the warp is wound on a kind of large wooden bobbins to dispose it for warping.

When the warp is mounted, the weaver treads alternately on the treddle, first on the right step, and then on the left, which raises and lowers the threads of the warp equally : between these he throws transversely the shuttle from the one to the other ; and every time that the shuttle is thus thrown a thread of the woof is inserted in the warp. In this manner the work is continued till the piece is finished, that is till the whole warp is filled with the woof; it is then taken off the loom by unrolling it from the beam on which it had been rolled, in proportion as it was wove.

To give woollen stuff the necessary qualities, it is required that the thread of the warp be of the same kind of wool, and of the same fineness throughout.

The woof is of different matter, according to the piece to be made. In taffety, both woof and warp are of silk. In mohairs, the woof is usually flax, and the warp silk. In satins the warp is frequently wool, and the woof silk.

The common weaver requires but little ingenuity in carrying on his business, but weavers of flowered silks, damasks, velvets, &c. ought to be people possessed of a considerable capacity: it is an advantage to them if they are able to draw and design their own patterns.

Journeymen weavers can, while in constant employ make a good living; they will earn a guinea and a half or two guineas a week, according to the substance on which they are employed. It is a business that requires no great

degree of strength, and a lad may be
bound apprentice to it at twelve or
thirteen years of age. Among weavers are frequently found men of a
thoughtful and literary turn. One of
the first mathematicians of this country was Mr. Thomas Simpson, an industrious weaver in Spitalfields.

The silk-throwster prepares by means
of a mill the raw silk for the use of the
weaver, he employs women chiefly. Spinning the hard silk and winding it employ
a great number of hands of almost all
ages.

THE STOCKING-WEAVER.

FORMERLY stockings were made of
cloths, or of milled stuffs sewed together; but since the invention of knitting and weaving stockings of silk, wool,
cotton, thread, &c. the use of cloth

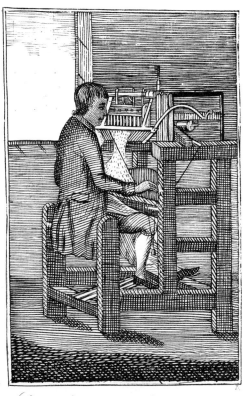

Stocking Maker.

stockings has been entirely discontinu-
ed. In the year 1561, queen Elizabeth
was presented with a pair of black knit
silk stockings, with which she was so
much pleased as to discontinue the use
of those made with cloth. It is said
also by Dr. Howel, in his History of the
World, that Henry VIII. commonly
wore cloth hose, except by accident he
obtained a pair of silk stockings. His
son Edward the Sixth was presented
with a pair of long Spanish silk stockings by Sir Thomas Gresham, and the
donation was highly esteemed. From
these accounts it should seem that the
invention of knit silk stockings originally came from Spain.

William Rider was the first person
who made them in England; and he, it
is said, learnt the art at the house of an
Italian merchant, and knit a pair of worsted stockings which he presented to William earl of Pembroke in the year 1564.

Modern stockings, whether woven or knit, are formed of an indefinite number of little knots, called stitches, loops, or meshes, intermingled in one another.

Woven stockings are manufactured on a machine made of finely polished iron or steel, such as that represented in the plate. It is of a structure too complex to admit of a description in this little work.

The invention of this machine is ascribed to William Lee, M. A. of St. John's College, Cambridge, in the year 1589. But by other persons the credit of it is given to a student of Oxford, who was driven to pursuits of industry through mere necessity. This young man, falling in love with an inn-keeper's daughter, married her, though she had not a penny, and he, by his marriage, lost his fellowship. They soon became miserably poor; and the only means by which they could support themselves were the knitting of stockings, at which the woman was very expert. Sitting constantly together from morning till night, the young man observed with great attention the motion of his wife's fingers in the dexterous management of her needles, and conceived that it was posssible to contrive a little loom which might perform the work with more expedition. They soon began to make the experiment, which completely succeeded. Thus the stocking-loom was first invented; by which the inventor not only placed himself above want, but has rendered to his country great and important benefits, stockings being a considerable article for exportation from this to foreign countries.

The loom has of course received several improvements, so that at length stockings of all sorts can be made on it with great art and expedition. By means of some additional machinery to the stocking-frame, the turned ribbed stockings are made as well as those done with knitting-needles. These, together with the manner of making the open-work mills, a curious sort of lace, aprons, and handkerchiefs, as well as a great variety of figured goods for waist-coats, &c., have sprung from the same machine, and form now a considerable additional branch of the stocking-trade.

Knit stockings are made with needles of polished iron, which interweave the threads and form the meshes of which the stockings consist. This part of the invention, as it is now practised, is given by some to Scotland, by others, to France, though it probably originated in Spain. In Paris there is no great house without its porter, and these porters em-ploy all their leisure moments in the knitting of stockings. In England knitting is not much carried on as a trade, but in country places most female

servants are expected to be able to fill
up their time in this way.

Knit stockings are much more durable than those made in the loom ; but
the time required for this work, espe-
cially if the materials are very fine, raises
the price too high for common wearers.
The Scotch are said to make the best
knit stockings of any people in Europe,
and they sell at enormously high prices,
from thirty shillings to four or five
pounds a pair.

The stocking-weaver requires more
genius than strength. It is a profitable
business to the master, but journeymen
must have considerable application to
earn more than a guinea and a half a
week. It is, however, clean, neat work,
and unexposed to the inclemencies of
the weather. They are paid so much
for each pair of stockings, and this varies according to the fineness of the

thread, cotton, silk, or worsted that is made use of: if however they do not possess a loom of their own, they allow the master two shillings a week for the use of his. Looms will cost from fifty to a hundred and fifty guineas each.

The hosier purchases stockings, night-caps, socks, gloves, &c. from the manufacturer, and sells them again. Some of them employ looms, and are in that respect stocking-weavers. The business of the hosier consists in being able properly to appreciate the value of the goods in which he deals, an art which is easily acquired.

THE CARPET-WEAVER.

THE carpet loom is very well represented in the plate : it is placed perpen-
dicularly, and consists principally of
four pieces, two long planks or cheeks
of wood, and two thick rollers or
beams. The planks are set upright, and
the rollers across, the one at top and the
other at bottom, about a foot or more
distant from the ground. They are suspended on the planks, and may be
turned with bars. In each roller is a
groove from one end to the other, in
which the ends of the warp are so fastened that all the threads of it are kept
perpendicular.

The warp is divided both before and
behind into parcels of ten threads
through the whole width of the piece.
The weaver works on the foreside.
The design or pattern is traced in its

proper colours on cartons, tied about the workman, who looks at it every moment, because every stitch is marked upon it, as it is to be in his work. By this means he always knows what colours and shades he is to use, and how many stitches of the same colour. In this he is assisted by squares, into which the whole design is divided; each square is subdivided into ten vertical lines, corresponding with the parcels of ten threads of the warp; and besides, each square is ruled with ten horizontal lines, crossing the vertical lines at right angles. The workman, having placed his spindles of thread near him, begins to work on the first horizontal line of one of the squares.

The lines marked on the carton are not traced on the warp, because an iron wire, which is longer than the width of a parcel of ten threads, supplies the

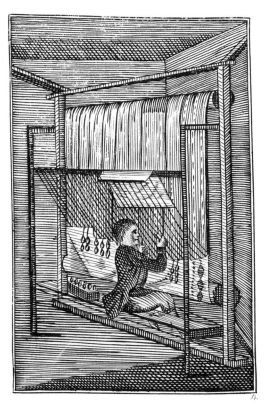

Carpet Maker.

place of a cross line. This wire is
managed by a crook at one end, at the
workman's right hand; towards the
other end it is flatted into a sort of knife,
with a back and edge, and grows wider
to the point. The weaver fixes his iron
wire horizontally on the warp, by twisting some turns of a suitable thread of
the woof round it, which he passes for-
ward and backward, behind a fore thread
of the warp, and then behind the op-
posite thread, drawing them in their turn
by their leishes. Afterwards he brings
the woof-thread round the wire, in order
to begin again to thrust it into the warp.
He continues in this manner to cover
the iron rod or wire, and to fill up a
line to the tenth thread of the warp. He
is at liberty either to stop here or to go
on with the same cross line in the next
division, according as he passes the
thread of the woof round the iron wire,

and into the warp, the threads of which he causes to cross one another at every instant: when he comes to the end of the line, he takes care to strike in, or close again all the stitches with an iron reed, the teeth of which freely enter between the empty threads of the warp, and which is heavy enough to strike in the woof he has used. This row of stitches is again closed and levelled, and in the same manner the weaver proceeds; then with his left hand he lays a strong pair of shears along the finished line, cuts off the loose hairs, and thus forms a row of tufts perfectly even, which, together with those before and after it, form the shag. Thus the workman follows stitch for stitch, and colour for colour, the plan of his pattern, which he is attempting to imitate; he paints magnificently, without having the least notion of painting or drawing.

The manufacture of carpets, after the manner of Chaillot, was introduced into London in the year 1750, by two workmen who left the manufactory in disgust, and came here to procure employment. They were first encouraged by Mr. Moore, who succeeded in establishing this important and useful mafacture, and who, in the year 1757, obtained a premium from the Society of Arts for the best carpet in imitation of the Turkey carpets. We have carpet manufactories at Axminster, Wilton, Kidderminster, Leeds, and many other places. It is a good business for the masters and journeymen, and now carpets are become of such general use, a great number of people are employed in the manufacture.

Another sort of carpet in use, is made of narrow slips of list sewed together; these of course are very inferior to those

just described, but they employ many
women and children.   A considerable
trade in the list carpets is carried on at
the Orphan Working School in the City-
road, an institution that does honour to
the liberality and public spirit of the dissenters in and near the metropolis.

LADIES' DRESS-MAKER.

The business of a mantua-maker, which now includes almost every article of dress made use of by ladies, except, perhaps, those which belong to the head and the feet, is too well known to stand in need of description.

The plate is a representation of a mantua-maker taking the pattern off from a lady by means of a piece of paper, or of cloth. The pattern, if taken in cloth, becomes afterwards the lining of the dress. This business requires, in those who would excel in it, a considerable share of taste, but no great capital to set up in it, unless to the act of making is united the business of furnishing the materials.

The mantua-maker's customers are not always easily pleased; they frequently expect more from their dress,

than it is capable of giving. " Dress,"
says Mr. Addison, " is grown of univer-
sal use in the conduct of life.   Civili-
ties and respect are only paid to appearance.   It is a varnish that gives a lustre
to every action, that introduces us into
all polite assemblies, and the only certain method of making most of the
youth of our nation conspicuous : hence
Milton asserts of the fair sex,

———————of outward form
Elaborate, of inward less exact.

" A lady of genius will give a gen-
teel air to her whole dress by a well
fancied suit of knots, as a judicious
writer gives a spirit to a whole sentence
by a single expression. As words grow
old, and new ones enrich the language,
so there is a constant succession of dress:
the fringe succeeds the lace ; the stays
shorten or extend the waist ; the ribbon

Ladies Dress Maker.

undergoes divers variations; the head-dress receives frequent rises and falls every year; and, in short, the whole woman throughout, as curious observers of dress have remarked, is changed from top to toe in the period of five years.

" The mantua-maker must be an expert anatomist; and must, if judiciously chosen, have a name of French termination: she must know how to hide all defects in the proportions of the body, and must be able to mould the shape by the stays, that while she corrects the body she may not interfere with the pleasures of the palate."

It will therefore be readily admitted, that the perfection of dress, and the art of pleasing the fair sex in this particular cannot be attained without a genius; the indignation expressed against those who fail in their pretensions is referred to by Pope:

Not Cynthia, when her *mantua*'s pinn'd awry,
E'er felt such rage, resentment, and despair,
As thou, sad virgin! for thy ravish'd hair.

The business of a mantua-maker, when conducted upon a large scale and in a fashionable situation, is very profitable ; but the mere work-women do not make gains adequate to their labour : they are frequently obliged to set up to very late hours, and the recompense for extra-work is not adequate to the time spent.   Young women ought, perhaps, rarely to be apprenticed to this trade unless their friends can, at the end of the term, place them in a reputable way of business, and can command such connections as shall, with industry, secure their success.   The price charged for making dresses cannot be estimated : it varies with the article to be made ; with the reputation of the maker ; with her situation in life; and even with the season of the year.

Mantua-makers work in silks, muslins, cambrics, cottons, and a great variety of articles, adapted as well to please the fancy, as for purposes of real utility. They require but few implements : these are chiefly thread, scissars, pins, and needles. Of the manufacture of pins and needles we shall give an account in the next article.

THE PIN-MAKER.

THERE is scarcely any commodity cheaper than pins, and but few that pass through more hands before they come to be sold. It is reckoned that twenty-five workmen are successively employed in each pin, between the drawing of the brass wire and the sticking of the pin in the paper.

It is not easy to trace the invention of this very useful little implement; it is first noticed in the English statute book in the year 1483, prohibiting foreign manufactures: and it appears from the manner in which pins are described in the reign of Henry the VIII, and the labour and time which the manufacture of them would require, that they were a new invention in this country, and probably brought from France.

At this period pins were considered

Pin Maker.

in Paris as articles of luxury; and no master pin-maker was allowed to open more than one shop for the sale of his wares, except on New-year's day, and the day before that: it should seem, therefore, that pins were given away as New-year's gifts; hence arose the phrase pin-money, the name of an allowance frequently made by the husband to his wife for her own spending.

Pins are now made wholly of brass wire; formerly iron wire was made use of, but the ill effects of iron have nearly discarded that substance from the pin-manufactory. The excellence and perfection of pins consist in the stiffness of the wire, and its blanching; in the heads being well turned, and the points accurately filed. The following are some of the principal operations.

When the brass wire, of which the pins are formed, is first received, it is generally too thick for the purpose of being cut into pins. It is therefore wound off from one wheel to another, with great velocity, and made to pass between the two, through a circle in a piece of iron of smaller diameter. The wire is then straightened, and afterwards cut into lengths of three or four yards, and then into smaller ones, every length being sufficient to make six pins ; each end of these is ground to a point, which is performed by a boy, who sets with two small grinding-stones before him, turned by a wheel. Taking up a handful, he applies the ends to the coarsest of the two stones, being careful at the same time to keep each piece moving round between his fingers, so that the points may not become flat : he then gives them to the other stone ; and by that means a lad of twelve or fourteen years of age is enabled to point about

16,000 pins in an hour. When the wire is thus pointed, a pin is taken off from each end, and this is repeated till it is cut into six pieces. The next operation is that of forming the heads, or, as they term it, *head spinning*; which is done by means of a spinning-wheel, one piece of wire being thus, with astonishing rapidity, wound round another, and the interior one being drawn out, leaves a hollow tube; it is then cut with shears, every two turns of the wire forming one head; these are softened by throwing them into iron pans, and placing them in a furnace till they are red-hot. As soon as they are cool, they are distributed to children, who sit with their anvils and hammers before them, which they work with their feet, by means of a lathe; and taking up one of the lengths, they thrust the blunt end into a quantity of the heads that lie before them, and catching one at the extremity, they apply them immediately to the anvil and hammer, and by a motion or two of the foot, the point and the head are fixed together in much less time than it can be described in, and with a dexterity only to be acquired by practice, the spectator being in continual apprehension for the safety of their fingers' ends. The woman in the plate is performing this part of the operation.

The pin is now finished as to its form, but still it is merely brass; for which purpose it is thrown into a copper containing a solution of tin and the leys of wine. Here it remains for some time; and when taken out it assumes a white though dull appearance. To give it a polish, it is put into a tub containing a quantity of bran, which is set in motion by turning a shaft that runs through its centre, and thus by means of friction it

becomes perfectly bright. The pin being complete, nothing remains but to
separate it from the bran, which is performed by a mode exactly similar to the
winnowing of corn, the bran flying off,
and leaving the pin behind fit for imme-
·diate sale.

The pins most esteemed in commerce
are those of England; those of Bour-
deaux are next; then those made in
some of the other departments of
France. The London pointing and
blanching are most in repute, because
our pin-makers, in pointing, use two
steel-mills, the first of which forms the
point, and the latter takes off all irre-
gularities, and renders it smooth, and,
as it were, polished; and in blanching
they use block-tin, granulated; whereas in other places they mix their tin
with lead and quicksilver, which not
only blanches worse than the former,

but is also dangerous, as any puncture made with pins of this sort is not so readily cured.

Pins are distinguished by numbers; the smaller are called from No. 3, 4, 5, to the 14th, whence they go by *twos*, viz. No. 16, 18, and 20, which is the largest size. Besides the white pins, there are black ones, made for the use of mourning, from No. 4 to No. 10. There are pins with double heads of several numbers, used by ladies to fix the buckles of their hair for the night, without the danger of pricking.

We shall now give a short account of the manufacture of needles: these make a very considerable article in commerce, the consumption of them is almost incredible. The sizes are from No. 1, the largest, to No 25, the smallest. In the manufacture of needles, the German and Hungarian steel are of the most repute.

The first thing in making needles is, to pass the steel through a coal fire, and by means of a hammer to bring it into a cylindrical form. This being done, it is drawn through a large hole of a wire-drawing iron, and returned into the fire, and drawn through a second hole of the iron smaller than the first, and so on till it has acquired the degree of fineness required for that species of needles. The steel, thus reduced to a fine wire, is cut in pieces of the length of the needles intended. These pieces are flatted at one end on the anvil, in order to form the head and eye. They are then softened and pierced at each extreme of the flat part, on the anvil, by a punch of well-tempered steel, and laid on a leaden block to bring out, with another punch, the little piece of steel remaining in the eye. When the head and eye are finished, the point is formed with a file, and the whole filed over : they are then laid to heat red hot on a long narrow iron, crooked at one end, in a charcoal fire; and when taken out thence, they are thrown into a bason of cold water to harden. They are then laid in an iron shovel on a fire more or less brisk in proportion to the thickness of the needles, taking care to move them from time to time. This serves to temper them, and take off their brittleness. They are now to be straightened one after another with the hammer.

The next process is the polishing. To do this they take twelve or fifteen thousand needles, and range them in little heaps against each other on a piece of new buckram sprinkled with emery-dust. The needles being thus disposed, emery-dust is thrown over them, which is again sprinkled with oil of olives; at last the whole is made up into a roll, well bound at both ends. This roll is laid on a polishing-table, and over it a thick plank loaded with stones, which men work backwards and forwards for two days successively, by these means the needles become insensibly polished. They are now taken out, and the filth washed off with hot water and soap: they are then wiped in hot bran, a little moistened, placed with the needles in a round box, suspended in the air by a cord, which is kept stirring till the bran and needles are dry. The needles are now sorted; the points are turned the same way, and smoothed with an emery stone turned with a wheel; this is the end of the process, and nothing remains to be done but to make them up in packets of 250 each.

Needles were first made in England, by a native of India, in 1545, but the art was lost at his death : it was, however, shortly after recovered by Christopher Greening, who, with his three children, were settled by Mr. Damer, ancestor of the present Lord Milton, at Long Crendon, in Bucks, where the manufactory has been carried on from that time to the present.

THE WIRE-DRAWER.

METAL wires are frequently drawn so fine as to be wrought with other threads, of silk, wool, or hemp; and thus they become a considerable article in the manufactures. The metals most commonly drawn into wire are gold, silver, copper, and iron.

Silver wire and gold wire are the same, except that the latter is covered with gold. There are also counterfeit gold and silver wires, made of copper gilt and silvered over.

The business of a wire-drawer is thus performed: if it is gold wire that is wanted, an ingot of silver is double gilt, and then by the assistance of a mill it is drawn into wire. The mill consists of a steel plate, perforated with holes of different dimensions, and a wheel which turns the spindles. The

ingot, which at first is but small, is passed through the largest hole, and then
through one a degree smaller, and so
continued till it is drawn to the required fineness ; and it is all equally gilt, if
drawn out as fine as a hair.

The next operation is that of the
flatting-mill, which consists of two perfectly round and exquisitely polished
rollers, formed internally of iron, and
welded over with a plate of refined
steel ; these rollers are placed with their
axes parallel and their circumferences
nearly in contact, they are both turned
with one handle; the lowermost is about
ten inches in diameter, the upper about
two, and they are something more than
an inch in thickness. The wire un-
winding from a bobbin, and passing
between the leaves of a book gently
pressed, and through a narrow slit in
an upright piece of wood, called a

Wire Drawer.

ketch, is directed by a small conical
hole in a piece of iron, called a guide,
to any particular part of the width of
the rollers, some of which are capable
of receiving, by this contrivance, forty
threads. When the wire is flatted between the rollers, it is wound again on
a bobbin, which is turned by a wheel,
fixed on the axis of one of the rollers,
and so proportioned, that the motion of
the bobbin just keeps pace with that of
the rollers.

Brass and copper wire is drawn in a
similar manner to that already described. Of the brass wire there are
many different sizes, suited to different
kinds of works. The finest is used
for the strings of musical instruments.
Pin-makers also use great quantities of
wires of several sizes to make pins of.

Iron wire is made from bars of iron,
which are first drawn out to a greater

length, to about the thickness of half
an inch in diameter, at a furnace with
a hammer gently moved by water.
These thinner pieces are bored round,
and put into a furnace to anneal. A
very strong fire is necessary for this
operation.

They are then delivered to the workmen called rippers, who draw them into
wire through two or three holes, and
then annealed a second time; after which
they are to be drawn into wire of the
thickness of a pack thread : after this
they are again to be annealed, and then
delivered to the small-wire-drawers.
The plate, in which the holes are, is
iron on the outside and steel on the inside surface, and the wire is anointed
with oil, to make it run the easier. The
first iron that runs from the stone, when
melting, being the softest and toughest,
is usually preserved to make wire of.

It is difficult to determine the period when attempts were first made to draw into threads metal cut or beat into small slips, by forcing them through holes in a steel plate. It should appear that as long as the work was performed by the hammer, the artists at Nuremberg were called wire-*smiths ;* but after the invention of drawing iron, they were denominated wire-*drawers,* or wire-*millers.* Both these appellations occur in history so early as the year 1351 ; therefore the invention must have been known in the fourteenth century.

At first, threads exceedingly massy were employed for weaving and embroidery : it is not at all known when the *flatted* metal wire began to be spun round linen or silk thread. The spinning-mill, by which the labour is now performed, is a contrivance of great ingenuity.

The wire first spun about thread was round; and the invention of previously making the wire flat is probably a new epoch in the history of the art: and it is a curious fact, that three times as much silk can be covered by flatted as by round wire; so that various ornamental articles are cheap in the same proportion. Besides, the brightness of the metal is heightened in an uncommon degree, and the article becomes much more beautiful.

The greatest improvement ever made in this art, was undoubtedly the invention of the large drawing-machine, which is driven by water, or by steam, and in which the axle-tree, by means of a lever, moves a pair of pincers, that open as they fall against the drawing-plate; lay hold of the wire, which is guided through a hole of the plate; shut as they are drawn back; and in that manner pull the wire along with them.

Wire-drawing in all its branches is profitable to the master; and to the workman it is a good business, being a trade that is not exposed to the weather, that can be carried on at all seasons of the year, and by which he may earn from one guinea to double that sum in a week.

THE PAPER-MAKER.

THE manufacture of paper is so curious, and so well worth the attention of young persons, that we recommend them to take some pains to get a sight of the whole process, which may easily be done wherever there are paper-mills.

Linen, such as our shirts are made of, is spun from flax that grows in the fields; and from linen rags, that is, from shirts and other articles of dress when worn thread bare, fine white paper is manufactured: of course every piece of rag, however small, should be preserved, and not thrown into the fire.

The first thing to be done towards the formation of paper, is to put the rags into a machine, or cylinder, formed of wire, which is made to turn round with great velocity to whirl out the dust: they are then sorted according to

Paper Maker.

their different qualities; after which they are put into a large cistern or trough perforated with holes, through which a stream of clear water constantly flows. In this cistern is placed a cylinder about two feet long, set thick with rows of iron spikes. At the bottom of the trough there are corresponding rows of spikes. The cylinder is made to whirl round with inconceivable rapidity, and, with the iron teeth, rends and tears the cloth to atoms, till with the assistance of the water it is reduced to a thin pulp. By the same process all the impurities are cleared away, and it is restored to its original whiteness. This fine pulp is next put into a copper of warm water, and here it becomes the substance of paper, and ready for the mould; for which purpose it is conveyed to the vat. This vat, of which we have a representation in the plate, is made of wood, generally about five feet broad, and two or three feet in depth. It is kept in a proper temperature by means of a charcoal fire.

The mould, which the paper-maker has in his hand, is composed of many wires set in a frame close together, and of another moveable frame equal in size to the sheet of paper to be made. These wires are disposed in the shape of the figure, which is discovered in a sheet of paper when we hold it up to the light.

The workman holds the frame in both his hands, plunges it horizontally into the tub, and takes it up quickly; the water runs away between the wires, and there remains nothing on the mould but the beaten pulp, in a thin coat, which forms the sheet of paper.

Another person, called the *coucher*, receives the mould, and places the sheet of paper on a felt or woollen cloth, during which the workman makes another sheet. They proceed in this manner, laying alternately a sheet and a felt, till they have made six quires of paper, which are called a post; such is the heap on the right hand of the vat. When the last sheet of the post is covered with the last felt, the workmen employed about the vat unite, and submit the whole heap to the action of the press, which is on the paper-maker's right hand. After this operation another person separates the sheets of paper from the felts, laying them in a heap; and several of these heaps collected together are again put under the press. They are turned and pressed several times, and then the sheets are hung up, three or four together, on lines to dry.

The paper is now to be *sized*, because

in its present state it will not bear the ink. The size is made of shreds and parings, collected from the tanners, curriers, and parchment-makers; and immediately before the operation a certain quantity of alum is added to the size. The workman then takes a handful of the sheets, smoothed and rendered as supple as possible, and dips them into the vessel containing the size, and when he has finished ten or a dozen of these handfuls, they are submitted to the action of the press; the superfluous size is carried back to the vessel by means of a small pipe. The paper is now to be hung, sheet by sheet, on lines to dry.

When the paper is sufficiently dry, it is carried to the finishing-room, where it is pressed, selected, examined, folded, made up into quires, and finally into reams. It is here submitted twice to the press; first, when it is at its full size, and secondly, after it is folded.

Every quire of paper consists of twenty-four or twenty-five sheets; that is, the larger number refers to paper made use of in printing: and each ream contains twenty quires.

In the manufacture many sheets are damaged; these, in the sorting-room, are put together, and two of the worst quires are placed on the outsides of the ream, called *outside* quires. The reams are tied up in wrappers made of the set-tling of the vat, and then they are fit for sale. Some paper is made smooth and glossy like satin, by means of hot plates; this is called hot-pressing. The process of papermaking takes about three weeks.

Paste-board is made in a similar way to that of paper.

Blotting-paper, and paper used for

filtering fluids, is paper not sized, in which therefore the ink readily sinks or spreads. Brown and other coloured papers are made of coarse or coloured rags.

Wove or woven paper is made in moulds, the wires of which are exceedingly fine, of equal thickness, and woven or laticed one within another. The marks therefore of these are easily pressed out, so as to be scarcely visible.

THE PRINTER.

THERE are three kinds of printing : one from copper-plates, for pictures, which we have already described* ; another from moveable letters for books, which is the subject of the present article ; and the third from blocks, for printing calicoes, linens, cottons, &c. This will be the subject of an ensuing article.

Of these branches, that of letter-press printing is the most curious, and the most important to the interests of mankind ; since to this art we are indebted for our deliverance from ignorance and error, for the progress of learning, the revival of the sciences, and numberless improvements in the arts, which would have either been lost to mankind, or confined to the knowledge

*See *Old-Time Crafts and Trades,* edited by Peter Stockham (Dover 0-486-27398-9), page 94.

of a few persons only. " To the art of printing," says Dr. Knox, " we owe the Reformation. If the books of Luther had been multiplied only by the slow process of the hand-writing, they must have been few, and would have easily been suppressed by the combination of wealth and power; but poured forth in abundance from the press, they spread over the land with the rapidity of an inundation, which acquires additional force from the efforts used to obstruct its progress. He who undertook to prevent the dispersion of books once issued from the press, attempted a task no less arduous than the destruction of the hydra. Resistance was in vain, and religion was reformed : and we who are chiefly interested in this happy revolution must remember, amidst the praises bestowed on Luther, that his endea-

Letter Press Printer.

vours would have been ineffectual, un-
assisted by the invention of printing."

The art of printing, in whatever light
it is viewed, claims the highest respect
and attention. From the ingenuity of
the contrivance it has ever excited mechanical curiosity ; from its connection
with learning and its influence on the
human character, it is certainly the most
important invention with which the
world has been benefited ; and young
people should endeavour to go through
a printing-office after they have read this
account of the art.

The workmen employed in printing
are of two kinds : *compositors*, who range
and dispose the letters into words, lines,
pages, &c. according to the copy delivered to them by the author ; and the
pressmen, who apply ink upon the same,
and take off the impression. In the
back ground of the plate a compositor

is represented at work, and a pressman is engaged at his business in the front.

The letters, or, as they are usually called, the *types,* are made of a mixed metal ; they are disposed in cases with separate square divisions, called boxes, for the different letters. There are two cases for the purpose of containing the types, called the upper and the lower case. In the upper are placed, in separate boxes or divisions, the capitals, small capitals, accented letters, figures, and the marks of reference : in the lower are placed the small letters, also the double letters, the stops, and the spaces that go between the words, and fill up short lines. A pair of cases for the Roman types and another for the Italic are usually placed on each frame, and they stand sloping, in such a manner as that every part shall be within the reach of the compositor. Having the letters properly distributed, he lays the written copy before him, and begins to compose. He has a small frame made of iron, called a composing-stick, in his left hand, in which he places the first letter of the first word of the copy, then the second, and so on till the word is finished ; he then puts a blank or space between that and the next word : in this manner he proceeds till he has finished the line, when he goes on to the next ; but all the letters are reversed, that the impression may stand right on the paper.

When the composing-stick, which holds several lines, is full, the compositor empties it carefully into a frame of wood called a *galley*. He then fills and empties the composing-stick as before, till a complete page be formed, when he ties it up with a cord or pack-thread, and, setting it by, proceeds to the next, till the number of pages to be contained in a sheet is completed : this being done, he carries them to the imposing-stone, there to be ranged in order, and fastened together in a frame called a *chase ;* this is termed *imposing.* The chase is differently made, according to the number of pages contained in a sheet ; that is, according as the work is folio, quarto, octavo, &c.

To dress the chase, is to range and fix the pages, leaving the proper margin between them : for this purpose the compositor makes use of a set of furniture consisting of slips of wood of different dimensions ; some of these are placed at the top of the pages, and called *head-sticks ;* others at the sides, called *back-sticks* and *gutters.* The pages, being placed at their proper distances, are secured by the chase and furniture, and fastened together by means of little

wedges of wood called *quoins*, driven
between the chase and the foot and side-
sticks with a wooden mallet and piece
of hard wood. In this state the work
is called a *form ;* and as there are two
forms required for every sheet, when
both sides are to be printed, it is necessary that the distances between the pages in each form should be placed with
such exactness, that the impression of
the pages in one form shall fall exactly
on the back of the pages of the other ;
this is called *register.*

As mistakes will occur, a sheet,
which is called a proof, is printed off,
and given to the corrector of the press,
who examines it while a boy reads the
copy to him, making the requisite al-
terations in the margin ; which being
done, he gives the proof to the compositor to be corrected. This is done by
unlocking the form upon the imposing-

stone, loosening the quoins and taking out the wrong or faulty letters marked in the proof, which he lays before him, with a slender sharp-pointed steel bodkin, and putting others into their places. After this another proof is taken, and, having been again read by the corrector, is sent to the author; who, if he wishes it, writes on it " *revise,*" which signifies that another proof is to be sent to him, to see that all the mistakes marked in the last proof are corrected.

Here then the compositor's work is finished, and it is committed to the pressmen, whose business it is to work off the forms thus prepared and corrected; in doing which four things are required, viz. paper, ink, balls, and a press. To prepare the paper for use, it is first to be wetted, by dipping several sheets together in water; these are afterwards laid in a heap over each other, and, to make them take the water equally, they are all pressed close down with a weight at the top. The ink is made of oil and lamp-black. The balls, by which the ink is applied on the forms, are a kind of wooden funnels with handles, the cavities of which are filled with wool, and this is covered with undressed sheep-skin, made extremely soft and pliable. The pressman takes one of these in each hand, and, having applied one of them to the ink-block, works them together till the ink is equally distributed, and then he blackens the form which is placed on the press, by beating the face of the letter with the balls.

The printing-press, represented in the plate, is a complex and very curious machine, which will be readily understood by any person who is witness to the operation. Besides the machinery for pressing, there is a carriage, containing a large and polished stone, on which the form is placed : this is rolled backwards and forwards to receive the sheet, and deliver it when the impression is made.

The form being laid on the stone and inked, the pressman takes a sheet of paper from the heap, and spreads it straight on a frame called a *tympan*, which confines two sheets of parchment and two folds of blanket between them; these are necessary to take the impression of the letters upon the paper. To the tympan is fastened, by hinges, a thin frame of iron called a *frisket*, which is covered with paper, cut in the necessary places, that the sheet, which is put between the tympan and the frisket, may receive the ink without injuring the margins. To regulate the margins, a sheet of paper is fastened on the tympan, and on each side is fixed an iron point, which makes holes in the sheet, and the points are placed in the same holes when the impression is to be made on the other side.

The carriage, containing the stone, form, paper, &c. is now, by turning a handle, rolled under the screw, which, with two pulls of the handle, performs the business; it is then rolled out again, and the paper taken off and laid on one side. The form is then again inked, and another sheet laid on as before; and this is continued till as many sheets are printed as the impression consists of. After one side of all the sheets is printed, another form, which contains the pages for the other side, is laid upon the press-stone, and printed off in the same manner.

In general there are two pressmen to each press; and then one man inks the form, and the other does the rest of the work. When the required number of sheets are taken off, the form is to be separated, in order that the letters may be restored to their proper cases. The form is first washed in a strong ley, by means of a stout brush, and then with fair water. It is then laid on a board by the compositor, who unlocks it, and, having loosened the lines, again washes it, to free it completely from dirt. When he wants the types to compose another sheet, he takes out several lines at once upon a brass rule, and taking a word or two at a time between his finger and thumb, replaces each letter into its proper division, and this is called *distribution*.

Besides the several kinds of letters used in printing, there are likewise *rules*, for black lines; borders; and head and tail-pieces. The rules for black lines are made of brass, and exactly of the height of the letter. Borders, flowers, &c. are ornaments in the form of long bars, serving for the divisions of books, chapters, &c. Head and tail-pieces are cut either in wood, pewter, brass, copper, or silver.

Journeymen printers, compositors and pressmen, will easily earn from thirty shillings to two guineas a week. The business of the pressman requires little genius, but a considerable portion of strength. A youth designed for a compositor ought to have been well educated in his own language; and he will find it of great advantage in the course of his business, if he understand something of the modern and the ancient languages.

THE BOOKBINDER.

Bookbinding is said to be the art of sewing together the several sheets of a book, and securing them with a back and strong paste-board sides, covered with leather. In this business, the first operation is to fold the sheets according to the proper form; that is, folios into two leaves, quartos into four, octavos into eight, and so on; this is usually the work of women, who perform it with a slip of ivory or box-wood, called a folding-stick: in this they are directed by the catch-words and *signatures*, which are the letters with the numbers annexed to them, at the bottom of the pages of the first one or more leaves in each sheet.

The leaves thus folded and laid over

Bookbinder.

each other in the order of the signatures, are beaten on a stone with a heavy hammer, to make them solid and
smooth, and then they are pressed.
Thus prepared, they are sewed in a sew-
ing-press, upon packthreads or cords,
which are called bands, at a proper dis-
tance from each other ; which is done
by drawing a thread through the middle of each sheet, and giving a turn
round each band, beginning with the
first, and proceeding to the last. The
common number of bands is six in folios, and five in quartos and octavos. In
neat binding a saw is made use of, to
make places for the bands, which are
sunk into the paper, so that the back
of the book, when bound, may be
smooth, without any appearance of
bands. After this the backs are glued,
the ends of the bands being opened with
a knife, for the more convenient fixing

of the paste-boards; then the back is turned with a hammer, the book being fixed in a press between boards, called backing-boards, in order to make a groove for admitting the paste-boards. The boards being then applied, holes are made for drawing the bands through, the superfluous ends being cut off, and the parts hammered smooth. The book is then pressed, in order for cutting; which is performed by a machine called a plough. After this the book is put into a press called the cutting-press, betwixt two boards, the one lying even with the press, for the knife to run upon, the other above, for the knife to cut against.

The book being cut, the paste-boards are squared with a proper pair of iron shears, and it is then ready for sprinkling, gilding, blacking, or marbling the leaves. If the leaves are to be gilt, the

book is put between two boards into a
press, and when the leaves are rendered
very smooth, they are rubbed over with
size-water ; the gold-leaf is then laid on,
dried by a fire, and burnishe off.

The head-band is now to be added ;
which is an ornament of thread or silk,
placed at the extremities of the book
across the leaves, and woven or twisted about a roll of paper.

The book is now fit for covering :
calf-skin is the most usual cover ; this
is moistened in water, and cut to the
size of the book ; the edges are then
pared off on a marble stone. The cover is next smeared over with paste, then
stretched over the paste-board on the
outside, and doubled over the edges
within-side. The bookbinder then fixes
it firmly between two boards, to make
the cover stick the stronger to the paste-
boards and the back ; on the exact per-

formance of which depends the neatness of the book. The back is now to be warmed by the fire to soften the glue, and the leather of the back is rubbed down with a folding-stick or bodkin, to fix it close to the back of the book. After this it is washed over with a little paste and water; two blank leaves on each side are then to be pasted down to the cover, and, when dry, the leaves are burnished in the press, and the cover rolled on the edges. The cover is now glazed with the white of an egg, and then polished with a polishing-iron. If the book is to be lettered, a piece or pieces of red morocco are pasted between the bands, to receive the title, &c. in gold letters.

The letters or other ornaments are made with gilding-tools, engraved in *relievo*, either on the points of puncheons, or around little cylinders of brass.

The puncheons make their impression by being pressed flat down, and the cylinders by being rolled along by a handle, to which they are fitted on an iron stay, or axis.

To apply the gold, the binders glaze the parts of the leather with a liquor made of the whites of eggs diluted with water, by means of a bit of sponge; and and when nearly dry, they slightly oil them, and then lay on pieces of gold-leaf; and on these they apply the tools, having first warmed them in a charcoal fire. When the gilding is finished, they rub off the superfluous gold, and polish the whole.

The business of the bookbinder, in general, requires no great ingenuity, nor any considerable strength of body. Journeymen can earn thirty shillings a-week; and much more, if they are good

workmen, and are intrusted with very
fine work. Formerly bookbinding was
not a separate trade, but it was united
with that of the stationer; it is now,
however, carried on alone, and bookbin-
ders are generally employed constantly
through the year.

The price of binding is regulated by
certain printed lists agreed on between
the bookseller and the bookbinder.

In the plate, the man is represented
in the act of cutting the leaves of the
book; on his right, on the floor, are
his glue-pot and paste-tub; behind
him are his tools for gilding; and on
his right is the press, for bringing
the books into the least possible com-
pass.

In London, the business of gilding
the leaves of books is a separate employment, and it is done before the

boards of the book are covered with the leather.

THE CALLICO-PRINTER.

CALLICO is a sort of cloth resembling linen, made of cotton; it takes its name from Callicut, a city on the coast of Malabar. The callico-printer is employed in printing this cloth. The first hint towards this branch of business was had from the Indian chintzes. The callico-printing was introduced into London in the year 1676, and it has since been encouraged by divers acts of parliament.

In the East Indies, they paint all their callicoes with the pencil, which they must do with great expedition, as the price there is very low; but here the following method is adopted: The pattern is first drawn on paper, the whole

Calico Printer.

breadth of the cloth intended to be printed; the workman then divides the pattern into several parts according to its size, each part being about eight inches broad, by twelve inches long; each distinct part of the pattern thus divided, is cut out upon wooden blocks; the cloth to be printed is extended upon a table; and the types, being covered with the proper colours, are laid on after the manner represented in the plate, and the impression is left upon the cloth. The workman begins to lay on the types at one end of the piece, and so continues till the whole is finished: great care must be taken that the patterns join with accuracy, and that there is no interstice or vacancy left.

Cutting the pattern in wood being the most curious part of the process, we

shall describe that particularly. The
cutters in wood begin with preparing a
plank or block of the proper size:
beech, pear-tree, and box are used for
this purpose; but the box-tree is the
most fit for the business, as being the
closest, and least liable to be worm-ea-
ten. As soon as the wood is cut into
the proper size and made very smooth,
it is fit to receive the drawing of the
design. Sometimes ink is used, and,
to prevent its running, it is rubbed over
with a mixture of white-lead and ·wa-
ter, and after it is dry it is rubbed off
and polished.

On this the design is drawn; and
those who cannot draw themselves,
make use of designs furnished by others
whose profession is to draw patterns.
The drawing marks out so much of the
block as is to be spared, or left stand-

ing. The rest they cut off, and take away very curiously with the point of exceedingly sharp knives, or little chisels, or gravers, according to the bigness or delicacy of the work; for they stand in need of no other instruments.

Block-engraving differs from that on copper, in this: that in the former the impression comes from the prominent parts, or strokes left uncut; whereas in the latter it comes from channels cut in the metal.

The manner of printing with wooden prints is easy and expeditious, if there be only two colours, as green and blue; or black, and a white ground, then the block requires only to be dipped in the printing-ink, and impressed on the cloth. If more colours are used, then they are to be laid on with a brush or brushes, and the impressions to be made as before with the hand.

When the whole piece is printed, the cloth is washed and bleached to take away any accidental stains it may have acquired in the operation : it is then dried, calendered, and laid up in folds fit for the shop.

Callico-printing is reckoned a very good business both for the master and his journeymen : the master, however, requires a large capital, a situation plentifully supplied with good and clear water, and extensive grounds for bleaching and drying their cloths. He employs three sorts of hands : the pattern-drawer ; the cutters of the types, who are also the operators in printing ; and a number of labourers, to assist in washing. The pattern-drawer is paid according to the variety and value of the designs ; and the printer, who is able also to cut with ability and taste, can, in the summer months, earn four or five guineas a week, or more.

A youth designed for this business ought to have a genius for drawing, a good eye, and a delicate hand. The business is not laborious, and the chief care is in the choice of a master who will do justice to his apprentice. Most callico-printers have some particular secrets in the preparation of their colours, which they ought to be bound to reveal to those whom they undertake to teach the art; since on the knowledge of this depends principally the success of the lad.

What are called wood-engravings are done after this manner, and so are paper-hangings, and playing-cards. But card-making is purely a mechanical business, and requires neither judgment, strength, nor ingenuity.

THE TIN-PLATE WORKER.

TIN-PLATE, or tin, as it is usually called, is a composition of iron and block-tin, not melted together, but the iron, in bars, is cased over with tin, and then flatted or drawn out by means of mills.

In the year 1681 tin-plates were made in England by Andrew Yarranton, who was sent into Bohemia to learn the art. The manufacture did not seem to answer, and was even reckoned among the projects called bubbles in 1720: in a very few years it was again revived; and in the year 1740 it was brought to such perfection, that very small quantities have since that time

Tin Plate Worker.

been imported. Our plates are of a finer gloss, or coat, than those made beyond sea, the ·latter being chiefly hammered, but ours are always drawn out by the rolling-mill.

The tin-plate worker receives it in sheets, and it is his business to form them in all the various articles that are represented in the plate, such as kettles, saucepans, canisters of all sorts and sizes, milk-pails, lanthorns, &c.

The instruments that he makes use of are, a large pair of shears to cut the tin into the proper size and shape, a polished anvil, and hammers of various kinds. The joints of his work he makes with *solder,* which is a composition of what is called *block-tin* and lead ; this he causes to unite with the tin, by means of rosin.

The business of a tin-plate worker is

very profitable to the master ; and the journeymen, if sober and industrious, can with ease earn from thirty-five shillings to two guineas a week. The principal manufacturers in London are Jones and Taylor's in Tottenham-court-road, and Howards' in Old-street. These seldom employ less than one hundred, or a hundred and fifty men each. Those who manufacture tin-ware on a smaller scale may be found in every part of the metropolis; and one of the chief sources of profit which these smaller tradesmen enjoy, is that of lamp-lighting.

This business does not require great strength ; but if a man would carry it on upon a large scale, it requires a very considerable capital : journeymen's wages may amount to between two and and three hundred pounds per week. In fact, the tin-plate worker pays his men twice a week; for on the Wednesday night a bell is rung, which announces to each workman, that the master or his chief clerk is ready in the counting-house, to lend money to those who cannot wait till Saturday night for their wages.

The large houses have constantly travellers in various parts of the king-dom; and, as they cannot carry the articles of their trade in saddle-bags, they have drawings of all works of taste, such as moulds for jellies, puddings, &c.

Tin in blocks resembles silver, but is darker. It is softer, less elastic and sonorous, than any other metal, except lead. It is easily extended into leaves, and melts more readily than all the me-tals. A composition of eight parts of bismuth, five of lead, and three of tin, will melt in boiling water. When tin is made pretty hot it will break with a blow. In the ore, tin is mixed with arsenic.

Tin, being less liable to rust than iron, copper, or lead, is advantageously used for the inside covering of metallic vessels. An amalgam of tin and mercury is used to cover the back surface of looking-glasses.

The chief tin-mines in the known world are those in Cornwall. It is a fact well ascertained, that the Phenicians visited these islands for the purpose of getting tin, some centuries before the Christian æra. In the time of king John, the Cornwall mines produced but little, the right of working them being at that period wholly in the King, as Earl of Cornwall. Their value has fluctuated at different periods : about a century ago they did not yield above thirty or forty thousand pounds per annum ; but of late years they have produced five times that sum. The Prince of Wales, as Duke of Cornwall, receives four shillings upon every hundred weight of what is called *coined* white tin: this amounts to about ten thousand pounds per annum. The proprietors of the soil have one-sixth, and the rest goes to the adventurers in the mine, who are at the whole charge of working.

The tin being to be divided among the lords and adventurers, is stamped and worked at the mill, and is then carried, under the name of block-tin, to the melting-house, where it is melted and poured into blocks or bars, and carried to the coinage town.

The coinage towns are Leskard, Lest-withiel, Truro, Helston, and Penzance, being the most convenient parts of the county for the tinners to bring their tin to every quarter of a year.

THE BRAZIER.

This artificer makes kettles, pails, candlesticks, and other kitchen utensils in brass. In the shops we often find, that the same people deal in brass, copper, and tin ware; and not unfrequently, the furnishing ironmonger sells almost every article made in brass and copper, particularly in large country towns. In such cases the brazier neither makes, nor is supposed to make, all the different articles in his shop; it is sufficient for his own purpose, as well as for the advantage of his customers, that he should be so much of a working brazier, as to be a competent judge of the workmanship of all the goods in which he deals. If he is a master in a large way, he employs a great number of hands in the different branches of his trade, and his profits are, of course, in proportion to the magnitude of his capital.

Some of the articles manufactured by the working brazier are beat out with the hammer, and united in their several parts by solder ; others are cast: those which are cast belong to the business of the *founder*, except the polishing and finishing, which require the art of the brazier.

The working brazier has need of strength, and, if he would excel in his profession, he should possess ingenuity, to finish his work with taste.

The *Founder* is employed in casting a thousand different articles in brass ; for which purpose he has models of the

Brazier.

work designed : to these he fits the
mould in which he casts his metal. He
rarely designs any thing himself, and
his chief skill lies in melting the brass,
and running it into the mould evenly.
There are various kinds of founders ;
some who cast for braziers only, others
who cast the different smaller articles
for coachmakers, saddlers, &c.; and some
cast the brass cannon, to carry on the
dreadful art of war.

The Founder requires a strong con-
stitution to undergo the heat of immense
furnaces : he may earn thirty shillings
per week ; but it frequently happens
that he spends a large portion of it in
porter.

Brass is not a simple metal, but com-
pounded of copper and zinc in certain
proportions : if the proportion of copper is greater, the compound is Pinch-

beck. Copper alloyed with tin makes bronze, bell-metal, &c.

Copper is dug out of the earth, or found united with many springs containing a portion of sulphuric acid. The richest copper mines in the known world are in the Isle of Anglesea. The mountain from which the ore is dug is called Parys; and from it have been dug thirty thousand tons in a year. There are two springs at Herngrundt, in Upper Hungary, so richly impregnated with copper and vitriolic acid, that iron thrown into them is dissolved by the acid, and the copper falls to the bottom in its metallic form. Near these springs, pits are dug, and filled with the water : old iron is then thrown into them, which, in about a fortnight or three weeks, is taken out, and the copper scraped off. By this process a hundred pounds of iron will produce from eighty to ninety pounds of copper. The same method is adopted at some springs in the county of Wicklow, in Ireland, and here twenty pounds of iron will yield sixteen of copper, which fetches a high price.

The Coppersmith makes coppers, boilers, and all manner of large vessels for brewers, distillers, and others. His work is very laborious, and the business is the most noisy of all mechanical employments. The wages of the journeymen are equal to the powers of body required in the operations.

Copper is used in a variety of the arts : but vessels made of it for culinary purposes are highly prejudicial ; for acid and fatty substances, when left in them any time, combine with the copper, and form verdigrease, which is an absolute poison, and when taken in the smallest quantities it is very prejudicial.

To prevent these pernicious effects, most copper vessels are well tinned on their insides. This operation is thus effected: The surface is well cleaned, by rubbing it with sal-ammoniac, or an acid; the tin, or a composition of tin and lead, is then melted in the vessel and rubbed well about it with old rags, doubled up.

The plate which accompanies this article represents a brazier working at his anvil: he has need of a forge as well as the smith, and, like him, his shop must be furnished with a strong bench, vices, hammers, pincers, and files of various kinds.

THE BUTTON-MAKER.

THERE are several kinds of buttons; some made of gold and silver lace, others of mohair, silk, &c., and others of metal. The plate represents a man who makes or stamps metal buttons only. The process is very simple, after the metal comes out of the foun-der's hands.

The pieces of metal are either cast or cut to the proper size, and then sent to the button-maker, who has dies or stamps according to the pattern wanted. The machine by which they are stamp-ed is well exhibited in the plate. The man stands in a place lower than the floor, by which he is nearer on a level with the place on which his dies stand : by means of a single pulley he raises a weight to the lower part of which is fixed another die; he lets the weight fall down on the metal, and the thing is done. After this operation they are to be shanked; which is performed by means of solder : they are then polished by women. At Birmingham this manufacture is carried on upon a very large scale. The late John Taylor, Esq. was the inventor of gilt buttons; and in his house buttons have been manufactured to the amount of 800*l.* per week.

Besides those cast in a mould, there are great quantities of buttons made of thin plates. The plates are brought to a proper degree of thickness by the rolling-mill : they are then cut into

Button Maker.

round pieces of the size wanted. Each piece of metal thus cut, is reduced to the form of a button by beating it in several spherical cavities, beginning with the flattest cavity, and proceeding to the more spherical, till the plate has got all the *relievo* required; and, the more readily to manage so thin a plate, ten or a dozen of them are formed to the cavities at once. As soon as the inside is formed, an impression is given to the outside, by working it with an iron puncheon, in a kind of mould like minters' coins, engraven indentedly, and fastened to a block or bench. The cavity of the mould in which the impression is to be made, is of a diameter and depth suitable to the sort of button to be struck in it; each kind requiring a particular mould.

The plate thus prepared makes the

upper part or shell of the button. The lower part is formed of another plate, made after the same manner, but flatter, and without any impression. To this is soldered a little eye, made of wire, for the button to be fastened by.

The two plates are soldered together with a wooden mould, covered with wax or rosin between, to render the button solid and firm ; for the wax or other cement entering all the cavities formed by the *relievo* of the other side, sustains it, prevents its flattening, and preserves its design.

The art of button-making in its various branches is encouraged and protected by divers acts of parliament. It is unlawful to import foreign buttons. And buttons made of, or covered with, cloth, cannot be worn, without subjecting the wearer to very severe penalties, if any person choose to sue for the same.

THE CABINET-MAKER.

THE cabinet-maker is but a superior kind of carpenter; he works neater, is employed on better materials, and his gains, whether considered as a master or journeyman, are probably much greater than those of a common carpenter.

All the arts of life have, no doubt, been the result of a gradual and progressive improvement in civilization. In nothing is this exhibited more than in an upholsterer's warehouse. What a difference is there between the necessary articles of furniture to be found in a cottage, and 'the elegantly furnished

house of a merchant or a peer! In the
former there is nothing but what is
plain, useful, and almost essential to
the convenience of life: in the latter,
immense sums are sacrificed to magni-
ficence and show. The cottager is con-
tented with a deal table, an oaken chair,
and a beechen bedstead, with other articles equally plain and unexpensive.
The wealthy possess sumptuous beds,
inlaid tables, silk or damask chairs and
curtains, sofas, and carpets of great
value; large looking-glasses, and bril-
liant lustres; together with a variety of
carved work and gilding. The furniture of a cottage, or of a small farm-
house, will cost but a few guineas; that
of a single room in the wealthy parts
of the metropolis, will be valued at
from five hundred to a thousand pounds.

The cabinet-maker furnishes chairs,

Cabinet maker.

tables, chests of drawers, desks, scru-
toires, bureaus, and book-cases of all
sorts and prices. But in almost all places the business of the cabinet-maker
is united to that of the upholsterer ; and
the furniture collected in one of their
warehouses is worth from ten to thirty
thousand pounds.   Such warehouses
may be seen in St. Paul's Church-yard,
Bond-street, and other parts of London.

The cabinet-maker represented in the
plate, is one that makes chairs, tables,
looking-glass frames, book-cases, &c.
His chief tools are, saws, axes, planes,
chisels, files, gimlets, turn-screws, hammers, and other tools, which are used
in common by the carpenter and the
cabinet-maker : but those adapted to
the latter are much finer than the tools
required by the house-carpenter. The
workman represented in the plate is in

the act of making a looking-glass frame; he is putting some glue on one of the side-pieces, in order to fix it in the hole that is prepared to receive it. The wood principally used by cabinet-makers is mahogany, which has been described under the article Carpenter.

Glue, which is of great use to the cabinet-maker, is made of the skins of animals, as oxen, sheep, &c., and the older the animal is the better is the glue. Whole skins are rarely used for this purpose, but only the shavings and parings made by curriers, fell-mongers, &c. These are boiled to the consistence of jelly, and poured into flat moulds to cool; it is then cut into square pieces, and hung up to dry.

The goodness and the value of furniture depend on the fineness of the wood, and other materials of which it is made, and on the neatness of the workmanship. A young man brought up to this business should possess a good share of ingenuity, and talents for drawing and designing; because much depends on fashion, and in pleasing the various tastes of the public.

THE SADDLER.

In early ages, when the horse was trained to the use of man, the rider sat on the bare back of the animal; but in the course of time a covering was used, which consisted of a dressed or undressed skin of some beast slaughtered for food. Such coverings became afterwards very costly; they were decorated with many ornaments, and made large enough to hang down nearly to the ground.

Six lions' hides with thongs together fast
His upper parts defended to his waist;
And where man ended, the continued vest
Spread on his back the house and trappings of a
     beast.   Dryden.

Sadler.

But it was reckoned, among the Romans, more manly to ride on the bare back than upon coverings; and Xenophon, in his Cyropædia, reproaches the Persians for placing more clothes on the backs of their horses than on their beds; and giving themselves more trouble to sit easily than to ride skilfully.

Saddles, as they are now made, are seats adapted to a horse's back, for the convenience of the rider. They consist of a wooden frame called the saddle-tree, on which is laid a quantity of horse-hair, wool, &c.; and this is covered over with tanned leather, neatly nailed to the wooden tree. To keep the saddle steady on the horse, the crupper is used, which passes under the creature's tail; and girths, to prevent it from turning round. To support the legs of the rider a pair of stirrups is

also added, one of which is very useful
in assisting to mount the animal : and
to prevent the saddle from galling the
horse's back, a saddle-cloth is commonly used. The articles made use of in
the manufacture of these things, are
more or less costly, according to the
price that the purchaser pays for his
goods.

Cutting-knives, hammers, and pincers, are the chief implements of the
trade ; that is, of the person employed
in the manufacture of saddles. To
complete a single article in the business,
the aid of many different artisans is required.

The tree-maker furnishes only the
wooden part of the saddle : this is,
however, a very important branch of
the business ; because upon the saddle-
tree the fitting of the saddle depends ;

and in cases when gentlemen wish to have their saddles fit properly, it is as necessary to measure the horse's back, as for the shoemaker to measure his customers for boots or shoes. The saddle-tree maker requires no great strength nor ingenuity.

The saddler's ironmonger furnishes him with the iron or steel stirrups, buckles of all kinds, bits for bridles, and other steel or brass furniture required for the harness of a horse, either for riding or drawing in a carriage. Many of these articles are originally made by the iron-founder.

There is also a distinct trade called a horse's milliner, who makes roses for bridles, and other articles used in highly ornamented caparisons. This tradesman should have an inventive genius, and a considerable share of taste to set

off the furniture belonging to a horse,
and decorate it in a neat and elegant
style.

The journeymen, in almost every
branch of the saddlery business, work
by the piece, and may earn a good living: they none of them require great
strength; the men always work in the
dry, and in most of the branches clean-
liness, which is no small requisite in the
mechanical arts, is a principal charac-
teristic.

The saddler makes all sorts of bridles, coach and chaise harness: of
course, besides the trades already noticed as peculiarly belonging to his business, he employs the tanner or lea-
ther-cutter; the currier; the embroi-
derer, who works devices, crests, and
coats of arms in gold, silver, or wors-
teds.   He buys broad-cloths and other

woollens of the draper, velvet and silk
of the mercer, ribbons of the weaver,
gold and silver and livery lace from the
laceman; buckram, thread, &c. from
the haberdasher. Of all these articles
he should, for the sake of his customers, be a good judge. The master
requires a considerable capital, if he is
in a large way, and called upon to give
much credit.

A great number of saddles are ex-
ported into foreign parts, particularly
to the East Indies, as English-made saddles are in great repute there.

There are many different kinds of
saddles, as the hunting-saddle, the
racing-saddle, ladies' saddles, &c. &c.

Saddles are of considerable antiqui-
quity: at Berne, about a century ago,
a saddle used to be shown as the same
on which Julius Cæsar rode; and in

the fourth century, the emperor Theo-
dosius forbad the use of saddles weigh-
ing more than sixty pounds.

THE GLASS-BLOWER.

THERE is scarcely any manufacture
of more real utility than that of glass.
It is formed of sand and salt mixed in
proper proportions, and melted in a
furnace.   Sea-sand is generally used
for the purpose, and the salt is an al-
kali procured from the burning of sea-
weeds.

The furnace is round, and has several apertures, in one of which the fuel
is introduced; the others serve to lade
out the melted metal.

Glass Blower.

When the ingredients of which glass is composed are perfectly fused, and have acquired the necessary degree of heat, part of the melted matter is taken out at the end of a hollow tube, about two feet and a half long, which is dipped into it, and turned about, till a sufficient quantity is taken up; the workman then rolls it gently upon a piece of iron, to unite it more intimately. He then, as it is represented in the plate, blows through the tube, till the melted mass at the extremity swell into a bubble; after which he again rolls it on a smooth surface, to polish it, and repeats the blowing, till the glass is brought as near the size and form of the vessel required as he thinks necessary.

There are three principal kinds of glasses, distinguished by the form or manner of working them, viz. round glass, as bottles, drinking-glasses, &c. ; table, or window-glass,—of this also there are several kinds ; and plate-glass.

If a bottle be to be formed, the melted glass at the end of the tube is put into a mould of the exact size and shape of its body, and the neck is formed on the outside, by drawing out the ductile glass.

If it be a vessel with a *wide orifice*, the glass, in its melted state, is opened and widened with an iron tool ; after which, being again heated, it is whirled about with a circular motion, till it is extended to the size required. If a handle, foot, or any thing else of the kind be required, these are made separately, and stuck on in the melted state.

Window-glass is formed in a similar manner, except that the liquid mass at the end of the tube is blown into a cylindrical shape, which, being cut longitudinally by a pair of scissars or sheers, is gradually bent until it becomes a flat plate. The best window-glass was, till within these few years, made at Radcliffe; but this manufactory is now abandoned, and the crown-glass is brought from Newcastle, as well as the green glass.

Plate-glass, for looking-glasses, is made by suffering the mass in a state of complete fusion to flow upon a table with iron ledges to confine the melted matter, and, as it cools, a metallic roller is passed over it, to reduce it to an uniform thickness.

Glass is sometimes coloured, by mixing with it, while in a fluid state, various metallic oxydes. It is coloured blue by the oxyde of cobalt; red, by

the oxyde of gold ; green, by the oxyde of copper or iron ; yellow, by the
oxyde of silver or antimony ; and vio-
let, by the oxyde of manganese.

Though glass, when cold, is brittle,
it is one of the most ductile bodies
known. When liquid, if a thread of
melted glass be drawn out and fastened
to a reel, the whole of the glass may
be spun off ; and by cutting the threads
of a certain length, there is obtained a
sort of feather of glass. A thread of
glass may be drawn or spun so fine as
to be scarcely visible to the naked eye.
Glass is very elastic and sonorous. Flu-
oric acid dissolves it, and the alkalis act
upon it.

Glass utensils require to be gradually cooled in an oven : this operation,
called annealing, is necessary to prevent them from breaking, by change of
temperature, wiping, &c.

The glazier buys the glass which he uses, at the glass-house, in crates, which contain twelve, fifteen, or eighteen tables each, according to the goodness of the glass: these he cuts to pieces or panes, with a diamond fixed in a ferrule. There are two kinds of windows, namely, those in which the glass is fastened in wood, and those in which it is fixed in lead: the glazier makes use of putty, a composition of linseed-oil and whiting, for the former: for the latter the lead is first cast into thin pieces fifteen inches long, and about a quarter of an inch thick; and then these are passed through a vice, which draws them out to the length of about four feet. The glass is fixed in grooves made in the lead, and the lead soldered together with a composition made of lead and block-tin.

Plate.glass comes from the manufactory in a very rough state; it is scarcely transparent. It is then ground with sand and polished with *emery,* which is a mineral substance, and *putty* formed of lead and tin calcined together. This last substance is the principal thing used in forming white enamels, and glazings for earthen-ware.

When the glass plate is polished, it is to be silvered for a reflecting or looking-glass, which is done in the following manner: A large and very even board is prepared; on this is spread very evenly some tin-foil, and on the tin-foil is spread quicksilver; the glass is then laid on the quicksilver, and a number of leaden weights, covered with baize, are laid upon the glass: in this state it remains several days, till the tin and quicksilver adhere firmly to the glass.

Glass-makers can only work in the cold months, owing to the great heats of their furnaces: their wages are large in proportion to the disadvantages attending their labours.

Glaziers, in London, make a considerable proportion of their profits by window-cleaning : the journeymen earn about four shillings a day.

Glass-grinders and polishers work by the piece, and may get a good living, considering that little more ingenuity is required than that which is necessary for common labourers.

THE CORK-CUTTER.

CORK is the bark of a tree of the same name. It is a species of oak. It grows thirty or forty feet high, having a thick, rough, and fungous bark : its leaves are green above and white underneath, and its fruit is an acorn, which is produced in great abundance. The bark of this tree is taken off by making an incision from the top to the bottom, and likewise one at each extremity round the tree, and perpendicular to the first. The old bark being thus detached, the tree still lives, and in six or seven years a succeeding bark is again fit for use.

Cork Cutter.

The bark when stripped from the tree is piled up in a pit or pond, and loaded with heavy stones to flatten it; it is then taken to be dried, when it is fit for sale. The tree is not in the smallest degree injured by the operation of peeling off the bark; for if it be not performed, it splits and peels off of itself, being pushed up by another bark from underneath. The cork-tree is found in great abundance in France, Spain, and Italy:—from these countries we receive the bark.

The cork-cutter's business requires but little ingenuity; the knives used in the operation have a peculiar construction, and they must be exceedingly sharp. The knife is almost the only instrument wanted in the trade. The principal demand for corks is for the purpose of stopping bottles; these are cut by men and women, who receive a certain price *per gross* for their labour. Cork-cutters sell also corks by the gross. It is one of the blackest and dirtiest of all the trades, and not very profitable either for the master or the journeymen.

Cork is likewise used by young people in learning the art of swimming; such are those represented in the plate, as hanging from the ceiling.

The cork waistcoat is composed of four pieces of cork; two for the breasts, and two for the back, each nearly as long as the waistcoat without flaps. The cork is covered, and adapted to fit the body. It is open before, and may be fastened either with strings, or buckles and straps. The waistcoat weighs about twelve ounces, and may be made at the expense of a few shillings. This article of dress would be very useful to all persons who travel much by water, or who are in the habit of bathing in the open sea. Cork is also used for the inner soles of shoes.

In Spain, cork is burnt to make that light kind of black called Spanish black, which is very much used by painters. The Egyptians make their coffins of cork ; and these, when lined with a certain resinous composition, preserve the dead a great length of time. In Spain they even line the walls of their houses with cork, which not only renders the apartments warm, but corrects the moisture of the air.

Cork, when burnt and reduced to powder, is often taken internally as an astringent ; and it has been said, that cups made of cork are useful for hectic persons to drink their common beverage from.

Fossil-cork is the name given to a kind of stone, which is the lightest of all stones ; it is fusible in the fire, and forms a black glass.

THE WATCH-MAKER.

This business has not been known in England more than a century and a half; but now the best watches in the world are made in London, and an immense exportation trade in this article is carried on here.

When watches were first made, the whole business was performed by one man, who was then properly called a watch-maker; but the name is now given to him who puts the various movements together, adjusts their several parts, and finishes the whole machine.

It is only about a century ago when

watches went upon cat-gut instead of chain; but cat-gut was materially affected by every change in the atmosphere, and of course the watch could not measure accurate time for two days together: but since the invention of the chain, and the great improvement in the temper of the springs, our watches are but little affected by the weather in this climate.

Watches and clocks, being adapted to the same purpose, are made or finished by the same artizan. The *former* are such movements as *shew* the parts of time; the *latter* are such as *publish* it, by striking on a bell. But the name of watches is usually appropriated to such as are carried in the pocket; and that of clocks to the larger movements, whether they strike the hour or not. Watches that strike the hour are called repeating-watches.

Watches and clocks are composed of wheels and pinions ; in the former there is a balance or regulator to direct the quickness and slowness of the wheels, and a spring which communicates motion to the whole machine : but in clocks, instead of the regulator and spring, there are a pendulum and two weights. The spring of a watch is inclosed in a barrel, on the outside of which is wound a chain : one end of this chain is fixed to the barrel itself, and the other to the fusee, which is a piece of metal in the form of a cone.

When a watch is wound up, the chain which was upon the barrel winds upon the fusee, and by this means the spring in the barrel is stretched ; for the interior end of the spring is fixed to an immoveable axis, about which the barrel revolves. The spring, being made of exceedingly elastic steel, endeavours to recover its former position, which forces the barrel to turn round; this motion obliges the chain which is upon the fusee to unfold, and turn the fusee. The motion of the fusee is communicated to a wheel, which, by means of its teeth connected with the pinion, turns another wheel, and so of the rest.

The parts of a watch are made by several different mechanics. The *movement-maker* forges the wheels in solid metal to the exact dimensions; from him they go to the person who cuts the teeth. This part of the operation was formerly done by hand; and perhaps one of the greatest improvements that watches and clocks ever received, was the invention of engines for cutting the teeth. This has reduced the expense of workmanship and time to a mere trifle, in comparison of what it was before, and has besides brought the work to a degree of exactness which no hand can imitate.

The wheels come back from the cutter to the movement-maker, who finishes them, and turns the corners of the teeth. The steel pinions are drawn at a mill, so that the watch-maker has only to file down the pivots, and fix them to the proper wheels.

The watch-springs form a trade of themselves : they are prepared by forming a very thin plate of steel into a double ring, bending it round with wire, and putting it in a proper furnace, to give it a suitable degree of heat. It is then dropped into oil or melted fat, which gives it a hardness equal to that of glass; it then undergoes several other operations to bring it to that fine colour and polish which it possesses.

The chains are made principally by women, who cut them at a certain and a small price per dozen. It requires no great ingenuity to learn the art of making watch-chains; the instruments made use of render the work easy, which at first sight appears very difficult.

There are workmen also who make nothing else than the caps and studs for watches; and others who make the cases, and others who cut and enamel the dial-plates. A particular set of tradesmen are called watch-tool makers, because their whole business consists in forming implements used by watch and clock-makers.

When the watch-maker has got home all the movements of the watch, and the other different parts of which it consists, he gives them to a finisher, who puts the whole together, and adjusts it to proper time.

All the branches of this profession require a considerable share of ingenuity, and a light hand to touch those delicate instruments which are requisite in their trade. The watch-finisher not only wants a strong sight, but is obliged to make use of magnifying glasses, the frames of which are adapted to the shape of the socket of the eye. Few trades, if any, require a quicker eye or a steadier hand.

The trade in watches is very considerable; of course it employs a great number of hands, and the profits of master and men are considerable. A man to be a scientific watch-maker, should understand the principles of mechanics, and something of mathematics; a lad, therefore, intended for this business, should have a mechanical genius and a good education.

Clock-making differs chiefly from watch-making only in the size of the works; so that a person who is conversant in the latter is equally fitted for the former.

There are many tradesmen in London, chiefly foreigners, who make a good living by the manufacture of wooden clocks; here every wheel, as well as the sides, is made of wood, and, excepting some wire and the striking-bell, there is nothing but wood that goes into the construction of those machines, which are sold as low as five shillings each; a very good one may be had for ten or twelve shillings. To these are

often attached *alarums ;* they then become useful for servants, to awaken
them in the morning.